The Practice Of Reality

Lillian DeWaters

(1883-1964)

Table of Contents:

THE PRACTICE OF REALITY

Ontology includes not only the true facts of Being but also their practice. Health, harmony, happiness, and the abundance of all good, are Answers which can be reached as we, the Self, think and act from our God-state, or standpoint of Perfection, as our All-in-all. By their fruits ye shall know them, is the Christ-edict for all time. Our daily experience of health, harmony, and the abundance of good, determines for us the exact extent of our spiritual Knowledge and exercise thereof: even as our success in mathematics is measured only by our ability to obtain correct answers to its problems.

Presuming that the reader of this work has studied the author's text book of Ontology called THE GREAT ANSWER, let us now summarize the Trinity of Being thus: I, the Self, am ALL. T include the perfect principles or facts of Being. I include perfect awareness and perfect activity. I include perfect body and perfect universe. Besides me there is none else.

We should understand right now that we are Totality; that nothing exists outside of us: there is nothing, therefore, which can or does oppose us. I am Self-Being-Spirit. I am one Infinitude, one Totality, one All-in-all. From this basis, we can see clearly that nothing is to be considered as originating elsewhere than in us.

Each one is I, since the "I" is infinitely identified. In everyone of us there is the same God-state (Father); the same right and might to think and act from the viewpoint of Perfection as everpresent and at hand (Son); the same light and illumination to be revealed (Holy Ghost).

Illumination has revealed that we should not continue to place "God" as synonymous with "Self," or "I;" but rather understand this word to denote the same meaning as

"Father," or our state of Perfection. God, the Father, is the first "person" of the Trinity. This God-Father represents Perfection, our perfect state of Being, Body and Universe. God is the very Truth; the Principle of Being which is immovable, incorruptible, absolute; that to which nothing can be added nor anything taken away. This God-Perfection is ever included in the "I" or us.

Will the reader please draw a circle on a separate paper, to be used for a definite and practical illustration. In the circle draw two horizontal lines so as to divide it into three equal parts. In the first space you may write the following:

I Am the Self. I Am the Father, God, Perfection. I Am the Absolute, Reality, Truth. I Am Spirit; Being; Life; Love; Mind; Creator; Body; Universe. I Am the One, Totality, All.

The second position of the Trinity is called the Son. This position of our Self is our activity; our consciousness or awareness; our free will. This is where we think, feel, see, hear, taste, smell, live and act. Presumably, we have all discovered that our Mind can think good thoughts or otherwise; we can "make good or create evil". Here, then, is the place of light and darkness; waking and sleeping; in fact, free will. Therefore in the middle space you may write the following:

I Am the Son. I Am consciousness; awareness; activity; thinking; feeling; hearing; seeing; tasting; smelling; living; loving; creating. I Am free will.

When we think and live from the standpoint of the God-state, that is, when we incorporate the Facts of Reality in our thinking and living, then our experience is one of happiness, harmony and wholeness. When the Father and Son, Perfection and consciousness, become one, this then culminates in the Holy Ghost, or spiritual Illumination, which is the third Position of the Trinity.

In the third space, you may therefore write the following:

It is we who have free will, not God! We, the "I," ever have the will to remain in the "Father's house", (think from the basis of Perfection) or not, as we choose. It is obvious that we are all doing this every day, is it not? When we are not dwelling in the God-state, but turn from it, it may then be said that we represent the "prodigal"; that we "sleep and dream;" that we function as "man." You see much choice as this could never be part of God: for "Thou (God) art of pure eyes than to behold evil, and canst not look on iniquity." (Hab.1:13)

Therefore, properly speaking, the "I" and "God" are not synonymous terms. We are the "I;" and all the while we are free to choose. We find that we think rightly some of the time, but not always. God, however, is always good, always Perfection, always Fulfillment, without beginning or end. Thus, God is our perfect state of Being.

When we function in the God-state, or state of Perfection, then we are in our proper position and in this State we see all things as they really are. This State always abides within us! We include, and are, ALL. We are the Circle; we are the Totality; we are the Triune One. When we admit only Reality, only Perfection, as our All-in-all, when we continuously dwell in the God-state, then our consciousness is the Christconsciousness, and is our Saviour. Thus the Christ is still our Redeemer; and our Deliverer from all darkness and sleep.

Perfect body, perfect universe, are ever prepared, finished, and at hand. However, until we think, act and live from the standpoint of the Truth, the perfect Facts and Principles of Being, we cannot consciously experience them; nor enter into the perfect Answer, which is Heaven. Perfect happiness and satisfaction can never be found in any other way. Thus, a partial acceptance of our perfect God-state, a partial awareness of our perfect body and universe, as ever present, and at hand, delivers to us a degree of harmony, happiness, wholeness and abundance. Ever our consciousness must expand and enlarge, in order that we rise from glory to glory, and so finally come unto the measure of the stature of the fullness of Christ, even as did our beloved Jesus.

I Am the Holy Ghost. I Am insight, revelation, I am illumination. I am the experience of my Self. I Am Christ. I am Heaven.

The general idea of the world before us is that it is external to us; thus it has been termed the world "without". Inasmuch as here appears discords, disasters, wars, and limitations of every kind, in our great and sincere desire to practice seeing only the good and the true, there was instituted the method of turning from this world to a world claimed to be "within"; and here was pictured a perfect and. ever harmonious universe, with no evil whatsoever. To repeat, desiring not to witness discordant appearances, there began the practice to turn away from the world altogether, and to create another world, free from all discords and limitations. although such practice may have helped and benefited many, now that a new light has dawned, we are to soar beyond it: for such a mental procedure assumes that the world we see and call "out there" is not the real and true one. Is this not so?

Now, then, when you sleep, and in your dream see a world of people, landscape, animals, and so forth, these are, of course, all within you, still you see them as though they were "out there," do you not? In like manner, the very people, animals, land, water, et. cetera, which you behold in your waking state, and have called the "without", are not external at all, for the simple reason that inasmuch as you are conscious of them, they exist in and of you; in fact, nothing that we see is ever external to us for we are the infinite ALL.

If one turns to an imaginative mental world as the Real and the True, what then about this world in which we eat and drink; this world wherein we work and play; act and sleep; this world wherein we see so much of beauty, grandeur and loveliness about us? In thinking most earnestly about this subject lately, suddenly, with light and glory, it was revealed to me that the world which has been termed the "without", is actually the real world "within us". I saw that any other mental world, so-called "within", is but imaginative: for since it is consciousness which sees, hears and enjoys this world, then this very world before us is the very world within us! The true world is ever with us, the Self. To the extent that we know the Truth about our Self, do we come to know the Truth about our world also.

Lo, this world wherein we walk, live, move and breathe, is the actual world, the Kingdom-of-Heaven world; in fact, the only Universe there is. Believing this world to be a picturing forth of all sorts of lack, discord and limitation, the tendency has been to turn away from it, even as Moses fled from the rod when to him it appeared as a serpent. Moses learned however that his own Being could teach him all things; that his own Being is all-knowing and Self-revealing: and so shall we all learn the same.

THE ROD AND THE SERPENT

In Exodus, fourth chapter, we find the revelation of the rod and the serpent. When Moses came back to the rod from which he had fled, lo, he saw there no serpent at all, but the rod only: he saw it had been a rod all the time. Similarly, never has anything but good been in our universe. Verily, this world, dear friends, the place whereon we now stand, is the City beautiful, the promised Land, the heavenly world, regardless of how we view it

When Moses fled from what he believed a serpent, he was actually turning from the rod, that is from reality. He needed not to destroy a serpent, nor unsee it, nor treat it, nor handle it. He needed but to bring himself face to face with the thing which appeared as a serpent, and right here, in this place, see the rod. This new point of view you will find to be the simple and pure reality.

There is but one world, and you, the Self, are seeing it, walking in it, enjoying it. This world of the Self is filled with beauty, charm, harmony, peace, loveliness, and all similar quantities. It is without spot or blemish; without war, discord or limitation of any kind. It is the universe of Spirit; it is the heavenly Land; it is Paradise.

How then shall one regard such appearances called war, discords, lack and limitations? The same as when one reports a serpent in a rod. First of all, let us recognize that the "serpent" (war) needs no direct treatment of any kind. Had Moses wanted to get rid of the serpent which he believed he was seeing, how foolish an idea to destroy it, pray over it, deny it, or cope with it in any other way. But how quickly and easily it vanished from view when we saw with the correct viewpoint! Thus we include Mind; but Mind is not a proper synonym for God.

The war of today is the result of imperfect and improper viewpoint of reality. It will vanish when the pure Principle of Being is more generally accepted and practiced. All the while Moses thought he saw serpent, he was actually seeing the rod, for it was this he was looking at. How foolish had he prayed to God to take away the serpent! Just as futile today to ask God to end the war. God includes nothing but Perfection; the same as in good there is no evil whatsoever; and in mathematics there is no mistake.

Any one of us may believe or say that 2 plus 2 are 5, but none of us can ever actually see it. From this simple illustration we can understand that incorrect answers to Life and Being may be mentally experienced, but never actually seen: such experience is like any dream. There are no events in a dream; no reality to it. All the time the Self, his world, and his true experience continue on, uninterrupted. The practice of the Self, therefore is its practice of Reality. The Self practices being the perfect Self, being intelligent, perfect Mind; practices living in the perfect world where there is no evil anywhere. In no other way can we practice the living Truth which we are, and function as the Christ-consciousness.

If one desires to know Perfection, he must see Perfection, and believe in Perfection as his All-in-all; he must see that his "earth is full of the goodness of the Lord." (Ps.33:5) Of course, the Self is the Lord. How could the wolf and the lamb, for instance, dwell together, and the leopard lie down with the kid, and the desert rejoice, and blossom as the rose, unless this were the way they really are today and ever? Perfection of Being is not a matter of evolution, but remains the same state "yesterday, today and for ever". "That which hath been is now; and that which is to be hath already been." (Ecc.3:15)

When we see from the standpoint of Reality or Principle that we are actually living now in the Kingdom, never having left it, and are ever experiencing our perfect state, regardless of any dream, then our report shall be, "Violence shall no more be heard in thy land, wasting nor destruction within the borders ... Thy people shall be righteous." (Is.60:18-21) Indeed, the "new heaven and new earth," which we are destined to see and experience as it really is, is not another dwelling place, but the same world seen in the correct way.

There is no such thing as two worlds, one without and one within us; one unreal and temporal, the other real and eternal. These are but two ways of looking at the same thing. To actually understand and accept this world before us as the genuine, the real and the true, brings one into a new sense of things altogether. Remember, the serpent was no part of the rod, and no more are wars, tribulations and vicissitudes part of our kingdom of heaven. As the real and the true are more fully accepted by us and more perfectly practiced, vain imaginations vanish. Thus to practice the Reality of Being, we, the Self, understand and act upon the Eternal Truth that this world before us is our real and true universe! This world before us, whereon our feet tread, is the very world within Us! There is no other!

"I go to prepare a place for you", said the incomparable Jesus. He paved the way; he illustrated the steps which we must take in order now and here to consciously see and experience the world which is indeed the universe of the Self. So our world before us will again appear free from war when we exercise our right and might to increase our consciousness of Oneness and Indivisibility. Then will spring forth a new and universal order of living, for all people. This new order will usher in universal peace, harmony and prosperity, virtually the Kingdom of Heaven on earth which for nearly 2000 years the whole world has been praying.

As Moses was led to see the nothingness of illusion, and the presence of the Real only, so, likewise, as we function in the Christ-consciousness, shall we all be brought into the knowledge and awareness that the Perfect is really all there ever is before us.

HEAVEN

Heaven, comprising, perfection, wholeness, peace, harmony, beauty and plenty, forever exists for one and for all alike, but must be discovered and accepted before one comes into an experience thereof. It is by no means merely a location where unlimited good abounds, yet such a heavenly place may be found right here, or wherever we are. All experience is Heaven to us to the extent that we exercise our spiritual vision, might and right to behold the Perfection of Being -- perfect Self, perfect body, perfect universe -- as everpresent and at hand.
The trite Metaphysical saying that, "Heaven is a state of consciousness", may infer that there is no perfect world, body, or Self, beyond one's awareness at the time. Such an assumption is altogether incorrect. Regardless of what our state of consciousness is, all the while the perfect and true world stands before our vision; we manifest the spiritual perfect body; we are the one and only Self and Being. We, the Self, the divine Us, the I AM THAT I AM, fill all space, and are Totality: there is none else.
Now, then, the way one looks at a thing, sees, hears and is conscious of it, may not at all accord with that is actual, real and present in his midst. Thus so long as he persists in the abstract statement that, "All is consciousness", he may be overlooking the supreme Fact that God, the Perfect state

of Being, including the perfect expression, body and universe, already exists in manifested form.

For instance, the real world before us is the real world within us; nor is it as perfect as one sees it; for regardless how he views it, it remains the finished Kingdom, at hand. It is free from evil; it is the land of Peace, Joy, Harmony, Beauty and Delight. "The generations of the world are healthful: and there is no poison of destruction in them, nor the kingdom of death upon the earth." (Apocryphal, Solomon 1:14)

Jesus declared, "The Kingdom of God is within you"! Here the Greek word for "within" is ENTOS, meaning in the midst. "For the Lord himself being asked by some when his kingdom should come, said, when the two shall be one, and the outside as the inside". (New sayings of Jesus) Verily, the Kingdom of God is our own Self and Being; and this Kingdom of good comes in our midst to the degree that we recognize and accept it as the only real and true experience there is; the everlasting and unchangeable Reality of Being. We, Self, possess all knowledge, nevertheless must experience this knowledge through our daily living: and this we do through our active awareness or consciousness of it. We might possess a fine automobile, for instance, but what value would it be to us unless it were put into use or into motion? Therefore, our correct use or practice of Mind determines our daily experience of health, harmony and abundance.

Neither our Mind nor body depends upon our state of consciousness! Our state of consciousness, however, determines the extent of the enjoyment of our perfect Self and body. We use Mind for thinking, the same as we use eyes for seeing. We are ever in a state of Self-knowing, termed consciousness; and this constitutes our daily experience.

To repeat; we are unconditioned Self and body; perfect, absolute, complete. Our Mind may report understanding or belief. Understanding is based on and represents Principle, Reality; belief has no foundation whatsoever, and is illusion. The nature of Being, or Self, is to enjoy and experience its wonder, power and glory; and this comes to pass according to the conscious awareness of itself as all there is. Such consciousness comprises its thinking, feeling, seeing, hearing and acting. Then the saying, "Heaven is a state of consciousness", rightly understood, means that our present experience of health, harmony, peace, success and blessedness is contingent upon our consciousness, on our present awareness of Peace, Harmony, Wholeness, Perfection, Love, Success, Abundance, Power and Glory as ever our very own; here, and in our midst; to be utilized on the instant.

We will never know all of our Self at any one time, since this would produce a state of limitation, whereas we are limitless because of our infinitude. The Self does not progress or expand; neither does its embodiment or expression. Consciousness does, however, in fact consciousness is continually expanding, as it rises from a boundless basis: and so our daily experience should be one of constant and uninterrupted progress and advancement in every direction. Said the Christ, "I am come that they might have life (be aware that they are Life), and that they might have it more abundantly (enjoy it in an ever-increasing manner)".

The Self abides in Heaven; the Self is Heaven. Harmony, love, happiness, is indeed the Nature of the Self; and for us to experience this Nature, is for us to experience Heaven. Real happiness, of course, is spiritual, that is, it is in and of such things as belong to Reality and Eternity; never to illusion or dream. For happiness to be real, and to endure, it must necessarily be founded upon purity, love and holiness.

Moreover we should know that never is it dependent upon certain people, times or circumstances; but is the Self's awareness of its own Wonder, Glory and Power. Thus our happiness cannot really be interrupted nor restricted in any way.

So long as we are conscious of discord or limitation, and accept it as real or true, we are not functioning our mind from the standpoint of Reality, but of the dream. In order to see and feel our Perfection as it really is, we must operate as the Christ-consciousness, the Mind that is without dream. True or Christ-consciousness can know no limitation or distress of any kind; ever it can have perfect confidence in its work: for knowing the Principle or Reality involved, it knows the result is assured. Therefore through our Christ-consciousness we come into our perfect experience called Heaven.

THE PERFECT BODY

The same spiritual viewpoint applies to the body as to the world. Our body is our expression, even as is our world. It is not an effect, but is Ourself, since we and our embodiment are the same One.

There is but one I-Life-Being; but one manifestationexpression-body. This, together with consciousness, comprises the Totality or Infinitude of Being. The one I-Life-Being is not divided nor sub-divided into separate parts, particles or individualities; but is infinitely indivisibilized; and its infinite indivisibility is its infinite individuality, ever operating as the Whole. Thus the body is one, yet infinite in expression: always the one Substance, the one Life, the one Being.

Ever the body is as perfect as the I AM; and as immortal, eternal and incorruptible. Any appearance of discord in the body is the result of improper viewpoint; and so, in his daily living, one experiences in accordance with his conscious awareness of that which is Eternal and True. One need therefore never treat nor handle the so-called sickness or limitation in any way, any more than he would attempt to alter the serpent appearing in the rod. Nor need anything be done to bring out health or harmony in the body, since always and ever it is present, and never could be changed nor affected in any way.

The act of Truth, which constitutes the treatment, is our awareness of the Self-body as it everlastingly is, -- perfect and immaculate always. My declarations and enforcement must be from this basis and none other! Really, no pain can or does exist in Being, and so no one is actually experiencing it; a dream is always nothing. There are no laws governing or controlling us but those we admit and sanction; therefore we should accept only the Law of Perfection, -- changeless and eternal.

Furthermore, we are to know and enforce the fact that there is no other false mind seeing, thinking or feeling any discord, as might seem to be the case; that we, the Self, have power almighty, and are equal to any emergency, since our ability to know Harmony and Immutability as ever intact and at hand, is everpresent, indivisible and absolute. I need to keep my Mind stayed on my Reality, my unalterable Harmony.

If I am conscious of some disharmony or discord, or accept it in thought (Mind), then I am living and thinking in a dream. Therefore in order to waken, I must begin at once to think and act from the basis and standpoint of my Reality. I must identify myself as the Christ-consciousness, the Mind which remains awake; and is not dreaming. Thinking as the

Christ-Mind, I soon find my peace, wholeness and harmony to be present, and intact.

While we dwell in the God-state no harm can ever befall us. Our consciousness of this almighty Truth, our awareness that we are the infinite One, constitutes our almighty power of deliverance; and "the gates of hell shall not prevail against it." (Mat.16:18) I, as the Christ-consciousness, can maintain and preserve my health, harmony and prosperity by thinking from the viewpoint of Reality. I know my body to be Spirit, or spiritual, never having been otherwise. Ever my prerogative is to uphold my Life and Being as omnipotent, omniscient and omnipresent, even as did our illustrious Jesus. This is the reason for my existence; this my destiny and eternality. The Self and the body exist as one Whole. Never should they be thought of as two, but always only as a unit. I, the Self, do not depend upon the body; nor the body upon the Self. These two are one Perfection, without shadow of turning; never to be evolved or developed, but ever and always existing as the perfect manifested whole. My body is perfect now; your body is perfect now; always Spirit, or spiritual. When we say that body is one, we mean that all body is the one Substance, the one Life, Self, Being. The one Self is infinitely identified as you, as me, and as all who are Life: so likewise is the one body.

Now, then, these facts about Ourself and body are not only to be known as Self-existent, but we are to enforce them, so as to experience their fulfillment in our daily living. It is not enough, for instance, that Mathematics exists in a perfect state, but we need to exercise or practice it in our mathematical problems in order to experience its ever-existent correct answers. Only our consciousness, or active knowing and enforcing of the Facts of Being, enables us to enter into the certain experience thereof. I AM! I must know that I AM! I must enforce what I AM!

Jesus knew his body to be Spirit, or spiritual; and moreover he also knew this to be true for others. Gloriously he proved to all, and for all time, that neither crucifixion nor the grave could take life from the body! The power dwelt in him, both to lay down his life, and to take it up again. Never did he believe his body to be at the mercy of circumstances. Verily the crucifixion and resurrection set forth the undeniable and irrefutable fact that the body is one with Life itself, therefore, ever immutable and incorruptible. Jesus' ascension climaxed his illustrious career; for he left no body among us. It vanished with him when he withdrew himself from us.

Thinking of some imaginative other body to exist within us, perfect and spiritual, instead of the very body which we are expressing at the moment, restricts our present demonstration of health and harmony as here and now. As this world before us is the perfect universe, and nothing less, so also this body with which we walk, live and have expression, is the perfect body, and nothing else. When this fact becomes more fully comprehended and enforced, the seeming limits of time, conditions, thoughts and beliefs will then have vanished.

The belief that there is a hidden other body somewhere to be brought forth, and that the body now visible and before us is not the real and true one, prolongs one's bondage and limitation today. As there is only one universe, and we are now living in it, so also there is but one body, and we are now expressing it. The correction therefore must be in our viewpoint, and never toward universe or body.

The notion that we are each an individual life and being, with an individual body, seems difficult for many to relinquish. First, it must be seen that we are not one of many, for I Am one Life-Being, the Whole, which is indivisible. The body, for instance, is composed of many different organs, nevertheless the body is one. So Life or

Being is composed of many different people, shall we say"
nevertheless Life or Being is one. When the word
"individual" is used, one is apt to think of some one or
thing separate from the whole. None of us can be separated
from the Whole. We are all the Selfsame Substance, Life
and Being; the selfsame "I" which is one Totality.
As, for instance, the blood courses through each finger of
our hand, yet is the same blood; and all the cells and skin of
the fingers belong not to the fingers themselves, but rather
to the body as a whole; so the Life which we are living, the
Principle of Truth which we are practicing, belongs not to
us as so many separate people or individuals, but to us all
as one Whole.
True, there are no two leaves of a tree exactly alike; yet all
leaves go to make up the tree, nor could a single leaf exist
apart therefrom. Naturally, we are as the leaves, that is, no
two of us are exactly alike, for the "I" of "Self" is infinitely
diversified, (or individualized, if you prefer to use this
word). You can see, however, that much of the so-called
"differences" are but part of the dream.
Certainly, it is true that we have distinctive talents, and that
we make use of our intelligence in various and
multitudinous ways. Paul expressed this idea very clearly in
his epistle to the Corinthians, 12th chapter. The entire
chapter is very illuminating ... "There are diversities of gifts
but the same Spirit ... All these worketh that one and the
selfsame Spirit". (4th and 11th verses)

I, THE SELF, THE ONLY CREATOR

In Isaiah, 45th chapter, 7th verse, we read the following
startling and arresting declaration: "I form the light, and
create darkness: I make peace and create evil. I the Lord do

all these things   A surface reading of this verse gives rise to the belief that God not only is responsible for all the evils in the world today, but actually creates them. Such a belief at once assumes evil to be as real as good.

Now, then, what is the meaning of the word "real"? It means to be actual or true. The meaning of the word "true" or truth is, to be constant, unchangeable, eternal. Therefore anything to be real must incorporate the qualities of genuineness, constancy, unchangeable and eternality. Reasoning upon such intelligence as this, can it be stated correctly that war, for instance, is real and true? Of course not! War began and war will end. The belief that it is real and actual but aids in perpetuating its appearance.

The Bible would group all evils under the word sin. According to the Bible as a whole, it is sin which is the root cause of all evil. It was Metaphysics that broadened this outlook, and introduced the idea that sickness, too, should be put in the same category as sin; also poverty and limitation of every kind. The next point of view must be to understand the meaning of the word evil. Even the great majority who consider sin, sickness, poverty, war and death as unrealities, nevertheless look upon them as evils. For instance, is it not a fact that you regard the war as evil? Do you not think of sickness, sin, poverty or limitation as evil? In fact, are you not regarding all forms of discord or limitation as evils which can be removed by Truth? Right here is where a deeper and more illumined perception or awareness needs to take place. A quickening of the Spirit is required which will permit a larger and fuller view of the baffling assertion, "I make peace, and create evil. I the Lord do all these things".

Just how can one truthfully declare, God is All, and at the same time regard sickness, sin, war or poverty as evil? Do you see what I mean? If, in your treatment, you assert that God, good, is all, how then can you also assert that war, for instance, is evil? Or how could you assert that it is real? On the other hand, how could you accept that "I the Lord make peace, and create evil"?

Today we, the Self, seem to hear about a war, do we not? We, the Self, (there is no other) seem to see sickness, disease, sin and various forms of discords and limitations about us. Is this not so? Jesus came into this world for a great purpose. What was that purpose? To rid the world of evil or evil appearances? No, for there seems as much now as then. To destroy anything whatsoever? Let Jesus, the Christ, answer in his own words: "I am not come to destroy, but to fulfill". (Mt. 5:17) "For judgment I am come into this world, that they which see not might see; and that they which see might be made blind". (John 9:39) "I am come that they might have life, and that they might have it more abundantly." (John 10:10) "I am come a light into the world that whosoever believeth on me should not abide in darkness". (John 12:46)

Jesus caused all kinds of sickness and disease to vanish, thereby proving they were neither real nor true. He spoke of some of these people as being possessed with a devil; other times he said they "sleepest". Still on other occasions, he set forth his understanding in a very clear and definite fashion. For instance, when Lazarus was considered by his sisters and others to be sick unto death, they sent word to Jesus, saying, "Lord, behold, he whom thou lovest is sick". Jesus' reply was, "This sickness is not unto death, but for the glory of God". Nevertheless "he abode two days still in the same place where he was".

At the grave of Lazarus, we find Jesus saying to Martha, "Said I not unto thee, that if thou wouldest believe, thou shouldest see the glory of God?" (John 11:40) Here he plainly alluded to sickness, and even death, as a place where the Self might be glorified. In fact, later on, in alluding to himself, he signified "by what death he should glorify God". (John 21:19)

At another time Jesus was questioned by his disciples regarding a certain man who was blind from birth. They said, "Master who did sin, this man, or his parents that he was born blind?" Here they wanted to discover the basic cause for this evil. However, Jesus replied, "Neither hath this man sinned nor his parents". In plain words, neither of them had committed any evil, therefore none was present. He then continued, "but that the works of God should be made manifest in him". There was only one reason in this case for the blindness, --- that here could take place the practice of Reality! The Self could here practice being God, being omnipotent and indivisible. Verily, our God-Perfection, Wholeness, Immortality, Indivisibility, must be practiced. For in what other way can the Self realize it is ALL?

I am come to show you how to practice being Perfection I am come that they which have not seen this Reality, might now see it; and that they which see sickness or trouble of any kind might become blind to it. I am come a Light, an Example, a Revelation into the world, that whosoever practices Reality should not continue in sleep, (darkness) but waken to Reality.

Perhaps all of us, at times, have thought of sickness, discord or limitation of any kinds as annoying problems or troubles; in fact as evils. But there is a much better and truer way to regard them. It was this very viewpoint that Isaiah was trying to convey to his people; that is, that we are the only Creator; that I, the Lord-Self, am ALL. Really, that which anyone may be considering an evil in his life, is but a place where he may waken to the glorious reality that Perfection is really all there is Never are there two opposing powers, good and evil. I, the Self, make good and create evil. I, the Self, am ALL.

In attempting to overcome war with war, for instance, of
course the darkness remains darkness. But think how the
Self might be exalted if only here, in this place, a new and
higher order of living were seen and established! Progress,
advancement, expansion, inevitably must come to pass,
since ever the Self must become increasingly aware of
Allness   Experience is the Self's fulfillment of itself.
Today there needs to take place a betters simpler, and more
universally higher type of government. It cannot be
prohibited; in spite of any nation or nations, it is coming to
pass. Wars need not take place; but if universal consent to
universal progress, expansion, betterment, is not
forthcoming, then war is the result. In this new light, can
you see that there is no evil power causing the war and that
though war seems such a monstrous evils still it need not
be if nations will but consent to national progress
expansion and advancement toward a new and higher order
of living in all directions?
There must come a new dispensation for all, which will
usher in a new and greater wealth, happiness, prosperity
and peace, than ever before dreamed of. The Self must
know itself Constantly and increasingly enjoy and
experience its majesty, power, wonder and glory!
Problems force the Self to function more and more from the
basis of Perfection, that is, from the true facts and
principles of Being. How could Reality be practiced if there
were no occasion, no necessity for the Self to ever
increasingly know and express itself? Such a necessity is
by no means evil, as is generally thought. Really, in the true
sense, there is no evil; but rather a place where the Self
shall be glorified: that the works of God should be made
manifest, in you, in me, in this nation, in that nation, over
all the world, everywhere.
Do you consider mathematical problems as evil? Of course
not. Moreover of what use would mathematics be without

mathematical problems? Similarly, how could Being enlarge its awareness of its perfection and completeness, its infinite good and harmony, if there arose no opportunities for expansion? No one regards mathematical problems as evil, but rather as essentials to knowledge.

The Self is omniscience! The Self should ever be expanding and advancing in the conscious awareness of its allness, its infinity, its almighty power and glory. Naught can stop, stay or hinder it, since naught but the Self exists. Said I not unto thee, that if thou wouldest believe in the oneness and allness of the Self, thou shouldest see the glory of God, the Self, expressed as Life more abundantly, everywhere?

Problems force us to expand our consciousness, and so participate in fuller and greater light. We should therefore cease thinking of problems as evils, and instead, know that since we created them, we can also dissolve them, and cause them to utterly vanish. The very fact that we (and not some other power) create them, is what gives us power to demolish them. Therefore cease to contend with some other force or power; use your Intelligence as power in the right direction. Nothing exists outside of you!

We may remain awake, and aware of good, or may partake of sleep, and dream of its absence. In this case, all that is needed is our awakening; an opening of our insight and perception to the fact that we have almighty power to let go the dream and again function from our real and true estate of Perfection, ever-existent, here, and at hand. When we sleep and dream, are we not still in our own rooms, safe and secure? No matter where we are dreaming we are, we are really only in our own rooms; our body is there, our life is there, our entire Self and Being is there In the same way, regardless of our dream of sickness, lack, war or limitation of any kind, we are living in the perfect universe; we are expressing the perfect body, and our God-Perfection has never been separated from us.

You may ask, How can it be true that I can think good, and evil; I can do right, and wrong; I can remain awake, and go to sleep, yet still declare," I am the Truth; I am God; I and my Father are one"? Again you may ask, I read that God is unchangeable invariable, absolute, without shadow of turnings therefore how can I reconcile myself with God? In only one way

by seeing that god means your perfect state of Being! The word God means Good, Perfection, Reality. Therefore, as light can never be darkness, so also Perfection is never imperfection. God is invariable and immovable. God includes the Perfection of the Self, body and universe. Reality never changes! It is without beginning or end. God is our Reality, unalterable and intact.

This fact I must prove for myself. I must find out all this for myself. This is the joy of my existence. As the answers to all mathematical problems are included in its principles, to be reached through intelligence and insight, so our answers, our fulfillments called Happiness, Health, Harmony, Peace and Prosperity, are all included in Gods our Perfections our Principle and Reality, to be discovered and experienced as we seek and fired, knock and have it opened, speak and have our word come to pass.

How much of mathematics would one know without participating in the solution of its problems? Little or none. How much of God, or Perfection, can we know and experience without bringing our hearts and thoughts into the awareness and recognition thereof? Little or none. While we sleep, we deprave ourselves of the awareness and activity of our waking states do we not? Yet in our sleeping dreams, we may waken ourselves to our normal state. Likewise now and here, while we seem to be confronted with problems called lack or limitation of any kind, we may indeed waken to our Reality, our perfect Self, body and universe, untouched by any dream; beautiful, luminous, irresistible. But we must so choose! We must so desire! We must so insist upon doing!

Jesus did it. He said that we can do it. Inevitably, we must. This time is now at hand; not only for people singly, but for nations; and for the entire worlds You will find the third chapter of Joel very illuminating. "Wake up the mighty men ... Let the weak say, I am strong ... Let the heathen be wakened ... Multitudes, multitudes in the valley of decision: for the day of the Lord is near in the valley of decision ... so shall ye know that I am the Lord our God dwelling in Zion".

Those who come into Peace and Prosperity shall be those who decide to burn to God, our perfects finished estate of Good, in every direction. Why call upon Gods our perfect state, to do that which is already done and finished? The principle of mathematics does not need to solve its problems. We, the Self, we alone must awaken, choose, decide, arise, come forth, return; and remain in our perfect state of consciousness which is the Christ!

Here we see aright; we see Perfection, God, as indeed All-in-all. We see that really we live, move and have our being in Cod, Perfections and never have we actually been severed from it. But as in a dream of sleep we may be dissatisfied, fearful and distressed, and our only actual escape from the dream would be to awaken from the sleep, so, also, our only genuine release from the dreams of war, discord and limitation is to awaken in consciousness to our God-state, our Perfect Self, body and universe as right here where we are; intact and everpresent.

Perfection is all. I, God, or the Perfect state, am the all and the Only, without beginning or ends Beside me, the Perfect, there is none else. I, Perfection, fill all space. To light there is no darkness. To Perfection there is no imperfection. To

Reality there is no unreality. "What concord has Christ with Belial?" (2 Cor. 6:15) How then can we reconcile light and darkness? The waking and sleeping states? We cannot!! All the time we sleep and dream, everything there is of us is in our waking state, -- our life, our intelligence, our body, our world. Now, then, in order for us to leave the dream, we should think of our waking state; this in itself will force an awakening. Therefore, if you are in a mental sleep, dreaming discord of any kind, turn yourself to your waking state, which is your perfect state, and think of it as your genuine Reality; and here you must dwell.

However, in order that we become aware or conscious of these existing facts, we must give up ignorance, false beliefs and their spectralities, and function consciously from the state of Intelligence and Reality. Do not place a scandal upon your Mind because it may think imperfectly, anymore than upon your eyes because they report the meeting of sky and trees. You would not place any blame upon your eyes in such an instance, and no more should Mind be considered imperfect because of false thinking. We, the Self, are the one who sees, hears, thinks Imperfect thinking must therefore be traced to us. We are above Mind; and above body. As we thank from the standpoint of our Perfection and Reality, we become aware of it, and so fulfill our Self and Being.

Always remember this; Our Perfection is God, really the one and only state of Being. We become aware of this God-Perfection to the extent that we believe in it, accept it, worship and adore it; lay down all thoughts and things for it; and come to claim and take possession of it as our very own.

Let us hasten to function in God, our Perfect state! We find David demanding of himself: "Awake why steepest thou, 0 Lord? arise cast us not off for ever". (Psalm 44:23) David is here speaking to himself; he is the "I" which needs to waken; he is the Lord, the one who can choose. David is not addressing God, he Perfect state of his Being, but arousing himself to function in and from that very state. Thus we are to return to God; return to Perfection in our every thoughts act and experience. When we do this, then indeed, we have returned to Zion, our real and true existence.

Here there is no sleeps no darkness; no dream. Here our consciousness is the Christ; and we are satisfied to dwell in this, our perfect state, for ever.

OUR AGELESS BEING

I am the Self with almighty power. There is none besides me; none to contradict or oppose me. How old is the Self? The Self was never born. The Self lives in eternity never having been separated from it. There is no time in Reality; and no time in a dream. The belief of old age is, in this new light, not an evil in itself; but rather it presents an opportunity for the Self to exercise, at this point, the awareness of its eternally ageless Being; timeless, limitless, unchangeable.

As the Self, we should think of our flesh as fair as a child's; and as firm and smooth. We should maintain beauty, grace and loveliness by becoming more and more aware of them as our own everpresent Allness, Perfection and Completeness. Actually, our body is eternally and uninterruptedly perfect in every way. When we entertain an improper viewpoint of it, we are as in a dreams yet, here we are afforded an opportunity to know the truth about the dream; that is, that in it no events are transpiring; no one is in a dream no substance, power, life or action exists in it.

Positively, we are to change our viewpoint from that of dreaming "age" to that of knowing the changeless, ageless loveliness of our eternal Being. The paramount Fact to know and enforce is that our body is Spirit, or spiritual, immaculate. Our spiritual body is ever safe and secure, perfect and absolute, unalterable and irresistible. No age ever touched it; no discord or disturbance of any kind ever interfered in any way with its purity, perfection and spirituality. No evil ever needs to be removed from it; no organs or functions set right; nor is any age to be added nor subtracted. Ever our body is beautiful as the morning stars and light as the sun.

CREATING OUR ABUNDANCE

Let us again bring before us the revelation of our Trinity, so that we will better comprehend just how we can supply our world with the things we would like to have expressed here. The first position of the Self is called "The Father"; the second, "The Son"; and the third, "The Holy Ghost". We may now set it forth as follows:

1. I am the First and the Last; I am the Totality of my world; I include the state of perfect understanding and perfect expression. This state of Being is called God or Father; meaning Principle, Reality, the Absolute, without shadow of turning, I am the Creator of my experience which, in order to be peace, wholeness, happiness and success, must be founded upon Perfection, Reality, God. Of course, I am Life without beginning or end; I am Intelligence; I am Power; I am the All in all.

2. I am ever in a state of activity and awareness of my allness and wholeness; this is called consciousness, the Son. I am continually knowing my Infinitude of Being; thus I think, see, hear, feel; and in all my various avenues of awareness come into the knowledge of my Self as all there is. Since I am all, I have free will to be a law unto myself. Functioning from my perfect state, (Father) I enact the Christ.

3. I am the fulfillment of my Self. This fulfillment, answer or true experience, is called the Holy Ghost; since only through my Self revelation and Self illumination, I come to express the Perfection, Power and glory of my Being. My creation is for the glorification of my Self ... that the Father, Perfection, may be glorified in the Son, true activity of Being. it is the Principle, Perfection, that I am, which permits and makes possible the works or activities of consciousness (the Son). Ever we should desire that Reality and consciousness, Father and Son, be one; since only in this state does the Perfect become known and experienced Our God-state, of course, is ever intact, and ever in manifestation. To the extent that we become awake to this ever-existent Perfection do we fulfill it in our daily living. Thus our knowing and our experiencing go hand in hand. If we consider the power of thought to be centered in something called Mind, we are depriving ourself of our own Sovereignty and Power; and are unawake to the Fact that I AM the First, and I AM the Last. All there is, including Life, Mind, Spirit, is in and of the "I" which is Alpha and Omega. We think; we live; we act; we feel; we love; and so on. Self revelation makes all these things clear to us; and this is why we should ever look to our own Self for all light, power and revelation: since looking elsewhere simply deprives one of inspired knowledge and the blessed experience thereof.

Creation is for the purpose of bringing forth the desires of
our heart in our daily living. Our experience, of course,
depends upon our consciousness, that is, our knowledge of
Reality, and our ability to hold steadfastly to it. Through
our illuminated awareness of God, our Perfection, we come
to express goodness, love, success and happiness. In our
present state of awareness, we feel the need for money,
home, food, clothing, etc. While such forms as these have
no eternal existence, nevertheless we have the right and
might to satisfy our desires at every point of our daily
experience, even as Jesus multiplied the loaves and fishes.
One must come to see that inasmuch as we are ALL, we
give to ourself and we receive from ourself. This giving
and taking constitutes our Self-existence and Self-support.
Ever before us should be the immovable Platform and
Axiom, -- Besides me, the Self, there is none else. For
instance, if you desire employment, who is to give it you?
None but yourself. If you have something to sell, who will
be your buyer? None but yourself. I am the one who sells,
and the one who buys. I am the one who gives, and the one
who takes. Through this activity, I am Self-supporting If I
wish companionship, who is there to supply it? None but Is
myself. If we deal with Mind, with people, as another, we
give to them the power which should rest only in our
hands.
Verily this is my dominion and authority, -- to govern and
control my experience from the standpoint that I alone am
its Creator. Who are those who come to me as my
companions, friends or associates? So far as I am
concerned, they are my consciousness; but to themselves
they are the Self. Until we see that our experience is but
our creation or conscious sness, we do not think of it as
such; nor recognize ourself as its Creator. Therefore until
one is fully awake to this Realism, he is, more or less, at

the mercy of his creation. Thus he may create a Frankenstein which later turns upon him.

It can now be seen that the "devil", "mortal mind", or "error", which in the past has received so much attention, has been nothing at all but one's own creations which, because not known as such, resulted in so much misunderstanding, havoc and tragedy. Whether or not we are aware of it, we are creating all the time; and until we do admit this liberating point, and take our position as the maker and creator of it all, we are at its mercy. Thus, no wander hopes have been thwarted, desires do not come to pass, and experiences fall so short of peace, harmony and prosperity.

One must look to himself! He is his Creator of good; he is his own supply of wealth and abundance, prosperity and success. As soon as one is willing to relinquish all other teaching, all other instruction, and all other beliefs, and seek only for his own Self and Being to be revealed to him, the illumination and revelation shall not tarry, but shall be found intact and at hand. Ever the Self must discover itself to be All-sufficient; Self-supplying, Self-sustaining; Self-existent. Thinking from this basis, this absolute Principle and Reality, we shall know the Self to be the mighty Father, the everlasting Saviour. Therefore "The redeemed, those who look to the Self to include Perfection, shall return ... everlasting joy shall be upon their heads: they shall attain gladness and joy; and sorrow and mourning shall flee away".

When we have allowed Ourself to be our Saviour, our All-in-all, then "The sun shall be no more thy light by day; neither for brightness shall the moon give light unto thee; but the Lord (your own Self) shall be unto thee an everlasting light, and thy God, (Perfection) thy glory. Thy people (Totality) also shall be righteous".   (Isaiah 60:19,21)

HEALING

What is healing? Is it the changing of conditions? No. Is it
the rearrangement of thoughts? No. Is it the adjustment of
dreams? No. Healing is one's awakening from sleep and
dream.

While it is true that there are no events in a dream; nor any
one in a dream; still it is true also that so long as I accept
any imperfection before me, I am dreaming. If I see
imperfection, or hear imperfection, or feel imperfections I
can do so only in a dream: I cannot do so in God, my
perfect state. if I believe that another is reporting sickness,
discord or limitation of any kind, I am forced to admit that
insofar as I am concerned, I am dreaming it; for it is certain
that all I know of another is my consciousness of him; and
were I functioning fully from my God-Perfection, I would
not be cognizant of imperfection anywhere. Thus it was
that after his resurrection Jesus did no healing works of any
kind ... He was then prepared to "return to the Father" the
state of uninterrupted Perfection.

Turning to Jesus' life while on earth, we see that "He is the
propitiation for our sins; and not for ours only, but also for
the sins of the whole world". (1 John 2:2) Indeed, how else,
except as his own consciousness could he have canceled
them?

He took upon himself the sins (dreams) of the world, to
illustrate to all how we are to prove our Reality of Being to
be ever present, and intact; and how our deliverance from
the sleep and dream is to take place. Surely while I sleep, I
can not enter into another's dream! Therefore, all I know of
anyone is what I accept of him in my own consciousness.
Thus, I should think of all others only as my Self; and from
the viewpoint of the One. Then I am free to see them

according to the standpoint of Perfection as my All and Only. I am responsible only for the way I see or view them. "He was wounded for our transgressions he was bruised for our iniquities; the chastisement of our peace was upon him; and with his stripes we are healed". So far as his consciousness was concerned, Jesus redeemed us. But so far as our consciousness is concerned, we are to redeem ourself; and not ourself only, but also the sins of the whole world. We are to learn that Perfection, God, is ALL.

It can be plainly seen that although Jesus healed multitudes of all manner of sickness, for instance, they were sick again; and died. In his world they were perfect; without beginning or end. To him, they were his people, the sheep of his pasture, characters in a world of which he was Creator. To themselves, they had free will to think, and to live as they chose: to discover their Perfection, at hand.

To myself I am all. I must deal only with my own consciousness. I must not believe in imperfections as existing in my universe. I must continually practice the thinking, feeling and acting that is based upon Perfection, Reality, Principle, -- my waking (God) state; the only real and true state there is. I must see another only as myself, the Self. I must refuse the imperfection that he presents. I must also refuse to believe that I am powerless to help him: for I have all power over my consciousness. "I am the Lord; that is my Name; and my glory will I not give to another". (Isaiah 42:8)

Jesus exercised power over all undesirable appearances, and spoke to his characters as he chose. Why not, since enacting his realization of Perfection as the All and only, he possessed supreme power over them? Right here we should recognize the infamy and depravity to rule one's world, and the people in it, from any basis other than that of infinite Love and Purity; from any ideal other than that of infinite Good and Harmony. To rule from another viewpoint is to depict imperialism, dominance, tyranny and personal dictatorship.

The 47th chapter of Isaiah clearly and vividly sets forth this erring position, and its doom. "For thou hast trusted in thy wickedness; thou has said, None seeth me. Thy wisdom and thy knowledge, it hath perverted thee; and thou hast said in thine heart, I am, and none else beside me. Therefore evil ... and mischief ... and desolation shall come upon thee suddenly".

The same book, 5th chapter, is also most illuminating for today. "Woe unto them that call evil good, and good evil; that putteth darkness for light ... bitter for sweet. Woe unto them that are wise in their own eyes, and prudent in their own sight!" Jesus unequivocally pronounced, "Woe to that man by whom the offense cometh". (Mat. 18:7)

To everyone, there is nothing but his own world; his own creation of consciousness. This is exactly what Jesus taught; and the basis from which Jesus functioned. He need not have been crucified. He could have stopped it at any moment, had he chosen to do so. However, he elected rather to prove himself superior to the experience called death; to come forth from the tomb whole and complete in every way. No wonder he later declared, "I am the first and the Last".

Is it not just that all responsibility or our state of consciousness rests upon us? In what other way could we ever hope to control our world, and our creation, except as its Maker and Creator? In this way only do we have power to cast out devils; to speak the Word and have it come to pass; to create a world without war, without sin, and without strife or struggle of any kind; to bring into experience the promised Land, the kingdom of Heaven; the crystal earth.

The greater our insight and illumination, the more perfect appears our universe of people, things and surroundings.

Finally our fulfillment has been brought to pass. This is our ascension.

FULFILLMENT

As the Self, we each write our own book of Life. Indeed who else could write our story? To take this enfranchising viewpoint is to simultaneously deliver into our own hands the key which opens for us the door of Paradise.

What is the "descent of the Holy Ghost"? It is the opening of our consciousness to admit the light of crystal clear understandingly --- the comprehension that we alone are the writer of our book of Life; that our experience is our own creation. "Tongues of fire" represent the outpouring of understanding from our own luminous awareness.

Reaching this Horeb height, we know that what we have made in the first place, we are able to change in the second place. "The Lord (Creator) gave, and the Lord taketh away". (Job 1:21)

As the Lord of our universe, we are therefore to bless our creations in every way; even as did our Exemplar. "Arise, shine, for thy light is come, and the glory of the Lord (true understanding of Being) is risen upon thee". To thy world thou shalt "Preach good tidings ... bind up the broken hearted ... give them beauty for ashes ... the garment of praise for the spit of heaviness ... For as the earth bringeth forth her bud

so the Lord God (the Self, enacting Perfection) will cause righteousness and praise to spring forth before all the nations". (Isaiah, 61st chapter)

As the perfect Creators we are to make the crooked, straight; and the rough places, smooth. We are to lift up our voice with strength; lift it up, be not afraid. As the perfect

Creator, we give power to the faint; and to them that have
no might we increaseth strength.

We, and our creation, shall mount up with wings as eagles;
we shall run, and not be weary we shall walk, and not faint.
Verily, we shall look upon everything in our consciousness,
(universe) and pronounce -- it is very good!

We, if we be lifted up from the viewpoint of a creation, to
that of the Creator, will draw all characters unto us,
Behold, I create new heavens and a new earth: and the
former shall not be remembered, nor come into mind, ...
and the voice of weeping shall be no more heard ... nor the
voice of crying. (Isaiah 65:17-19)

Imperishable beauty, harmony, glory, are ever mine as the
perfect One. Here, I include and express all that is pure,
good and enduring. My Principle of Being is Perfection,
and nothing less. Operating this Principle, this Perfection, I
lift the veil of mystery from myself and creation, and bring
my Sovereignty to light.

Perfection is the reality of all things. It is the Alpha and
Omega of Being. Ever our Christ-consciousness can prove
this to be the fact of existence, everywhere. I Am perfect
love, perfect light, perfect understanding. I Am the
Substance of all; the Spirit that quickeneth; the I AM that I
AM.

Principle and Reality, God and Father, denote our perfect
state of Being; our pure intelligence; our immaculate body;
our perfect universe: intact, at hand; now and always.
Therefore let us think, live and act from our awareness of
Perfection as the All and Only. Verily, we are the God
which fills all space ... the divine Us ... the Totality of
Being.

"Let him that is athirst, come. And whosoever will, let him
take the water of Life freely". (Rev. 22:17) Whosoever
will, let him begin now, this very day, to write his book of
Life from the standpoint of Perfection as his All and Only.

This is THE PRACTICE OF REALITY.

Lillian DeWaters

Made in United States
Troutdale, OR
04/25/2024

19452103R00024